I0109144

Footnotes to Life

Also by Rohit (Roy) Kajaria

A Constitution for a Democracy (An excursion in nonfiction)

Footnotes to Life

An Emotional Meandering

Rohit Kajaria

RESOURCE *Publications* · Eugene, Oregon

FOOTNOTES TO LIFE
An Emotional Meandering

Copyright © 2024 Rohit Kajaria. All rights reserved. Except for brief quotations in critical publications or reviews, no part of this book may be reproduced in any manner without prior written permission from the publisher. Write: Permissions, Wipf and Stock Publishers, 199 W. 8th Ave., Suite 3, Eugene, OR 97401.

Resource Publications
An Imprint of Wipf and Stock Publishers
199 W. 8th Ave., Suite 3
Eugene, OR 97401

www.wipfandstock.com

PAPERBACK ISBN: 978-1-4982-09731
HARDCOVER ISBN: 978-1-4982-0975-5
EBOOK ISBN: 978-1-4982-0974-8

VERSION NUMBER 05/15/24

For my daughter Nina,
With love

CONTENTS

MY POEM

Dear reader
please read my poem
with your heart and not your head,
for it comes straight from my heart
to this piece of paper
bypassing my head
as I sing the blues & jazz of existence
in my voice.
Please do not smash my poem
with the sledgehammer of your logic
or dissect it with precise analysis,
for it is not an engineering textbook
with mathematical formulas,
an income statement with profit and loss,
or a balance sheet with assets and liabilities.
Please do not stifle it with a rigorous format,
or suffocate it with the rules of grammar.
For it is a free-flowing river,
sometimes calm and deep,
sometimes shallow and turbulent
that flows from my heart to yours,
not controlled by dams of rhythm and rhyme.
Just swim with the flow

and ride the rapids
to enjoy the poetic freedom
of an emotional meandering
for what it is worth
as a footnote to life.

UNTITLED

Like the Roman aqueduct
two thousand years old
standing without mortar
that delivered water
over a perfect gradient.
Like the chisel of a sculptor
being hammered
into amorphous marble
at the birth pangs
of a beautiful statue.
Like the brush of a painter
dipped in viscous oil
mixing paints
being splashed on canvas
in a mix of
red, blue, green, and yellow.
Like the wrinkles on your trembling hands
laying bricks on top of cement
wiping perspiration with patience
to build the foundation of my life
in the scorching heat of a desert journey.
Like the tears flowing down a river
that merges into a sea of laughter

you wiped my tears with yours
and dissolved your laughter into mine.
Like the ballerina on a dance floor
like a figure skater on ice
you made it look so easy to the innocent eye
wrapping love in discipline
and discipline in love
so your boy wouldn't stumble
on the cobblestones of life.
Like the flooded river
your sacrifice with no limits
like a work of modern art
your love too diffuse to condense
into the fictional definition of a title
is untitled.

MA[1]

With you living in heaven
and me in the secular universe
the only place I can meet you
is at the fictional intersection of the two.
I am sorry I did not travel ten thousand miles
to pay my last respects
as you passed on
with my name on your lips.
I hope you understood that
vultures that devour
their flesh and blood
kept me away from you.
Ready to pounce on love and emotions
they wanted to kill
innocence with guile
and violate our love
in the name of love
with an emotional web
wrapped in guilt.
I could not afford
to let my heart rule my head.
In the interest of survival

1. Ma was my maternal grandmother who raised me.

the only way to deal with vultures
was to remain distant and invisible
where they could not reach me.
Even though
I loved you with all my heart,
I could not reciprocate
your unconditional love.
I can never pay you back
what I owe in tender loving care.
Now that the vultures are gone
so are you
and my desire to see you
has no anchor in reality
since I cannot be where you are
and you cannot be where I am.
The only way I can apologize
is to explain my behavior
that hurt your feelings
in person
at the midpoint of fiction and nonfiction
dream and reality.
At the intersection of heaven
and the secular universe
I would like to comfort you
with hugs and kisses
as tears after the fact
wipe the ones before
in an afterthought
of a footnote to life.

PROMISE

Do you remember the promise you made, my boy,
before flying on a ten-thousand-mile journey
that would take you away forever
where I could never touch you.
It was the promise to visit me once
before I left the earth
to give me a final hug and a final kiss,
to share the last tear and the last laugh
that I could take with me as a memento.
You were my pride and joy, my boy,
and the apple of my eye.
I looked at you as Michelangelo looked at David
and as Picasso looked at Guernica.
With the last kiss at the Bombay Airport
I was so happy and proud to see you go
as the finished product of my diligence
to realize your dreams in a foreign land
and to embark on a new life.
Now that I am old and near-death
I want to meet you in any corner of the world
but you do not want to be with me,
I do not know why.
It hurts my feelings and breaks my heart

despite your reasons
no matter how well-founded.
Since you do not want to see me, my son,
I have no choice but to pass away
with your name on my lips
as I long for you
to the last breath of my life
until I am no more
lost in an abyss.

SEARCH

(Looking for Ma in a posthumous fog)
In the wrinkles of an old waitress
pouring coffee in my cup
with her trembling hand
instead of spoiling her grandchildren
with hugs and kisses,
I look for you.
In the solitude shattered
by a sledgehammer of noise
that scatters my thoughts,
I look for you.
In the mirage of time slipping from my fingers
that keeps flowing
that I am too helpless to stop,
I look for you.
At the boundary of fact and fiction
that is hard to discern with a naked eye,
I look for you.
In the foregone conclusions of life
that could have been otherwise
for better or for worse,
I look for you.
In the broken dreams and distorted lives

with warped faces
screaming for help,
I look for you.
In the irrelevant regrets of love
lost in a smoke ring and a glass of beer,
I look for you.
In the last roar of a brave lion
shot down by a timid bullet,
I look for you.
In the tears and laughter
we shared and then missed
about tragedies and comedies,
I look for you.
In all the stories you wanted to tell me
of the tough breaks and hard times
before and after I left,
I look for you.
In a cup of coffee in a restaurant
where we could talk about old times and new
with nothing to add and nothing to subtract,
I look for you.
In the tea, you brewed for me
and poured with love every day,
I look for you.
At the intersection of day and night, secular and divine,
finite and infinite, possible and impossible,
I look for you.
Before life dissolves into oblivion
without leaving a trace of me
at the edge of an abyss
believe me, Ma,
I look for you.

FIGHT

Like the roar of a lion
shot down by a treacherous bullet
I want to fight.
Every time I fall down
Ma whispers in my ear
don't lose courage, my son
don't ever lose courage, my boy.
So, I get up and start fighting
to be true to her whisper
wrapped in an axiomatic faith
I want to fight.
I do not know
how to make a difference
or how to matter
without fighting.
So, for human life to be
more than a dog
pissing on a tomb
in an existential mockery
I want to fight.
Fate, inequity, unfairness
the stranglehold on humanity
I want to fight.

At the intersection of courage and cowardice
deception and honesty
discretion and indiscretion
vulgarity and decency
lies and truth
I want to fight.
I want to stare history in the face
and ask her
why she was always written
by the cowardice of the winner,
not the courage of the loser,
by the duplicity of the winner,
not the honesty of the loser,
by the indiscretion of the winner,
not the discretion of the loser,
by the vulgarity of the winner,
not the decency of the loser,
by the lie of the winner,
not the truth of the loser.
To be fair to the lion
I want to rewrite history.
I want to listen to his roar,
and synchronize with his footsteps.
To change history
I want to feel like a lion,
and chase down the hunter
to challenge him to a duel
face to face
one on one
fair and square
settle the score.

For I want to fight.
If you see me
lying in a ditch
on the side of the road
with mud and blood
all over my face
tired of walking
and fighting
when I fall asleep
at twilight
please wake me up
and remind me of how far I have to go
to keep the promises I made
when I was still young.
I want to keep walking
and keep fighting
until I reach the light of dawn
nuanced in humanity
to the last drop of my blood
and to the last breath,
until her whisper fades from my ear
under a fictional paradigm of bravery
I want to fight.

ROMA

(A fictional extrapolation of a real journey)

I want to feel history.

At dawn, I studied and analyzed history. At dusk, I want to feel history.

From dark valleys of barbarism to breathtaking heights of humanity, I want to swing with the pendulum of history.

For I want to feel history.

I want to ask Romulus why he killed his twin brother Remus, who was raised with him by their she-wolf mother. I want to hear the Etruscan rites he chanted while founding Rome in 753 BC.

I want to feel history.

I want to march with Scipio Africanus into the Roman Forum after he defeated Hannibal at the battle of Zama in 202 BC, and then whisper in his ear *memento mori*—remember death.

After every speech, I want to shout with Cato, the elder, "*Delenda est Carthago*—Carthage must be destroyed."

After the third Punic war in 146 BC, I want to burn Carthage to the ground with Scipio Aemilianus and curse her with salt. Then I want to wipe his tears as he wept over the death and destruction he had caused.

I want to discuss the Roman constitution with Polybius.

I want to feel history.

I want to comfort Cornelia Africana in her lament that she is well known as the daughter of Scipio Africanus, but not as the mother of Tiberius and Gaius Gracchus.

I want to protect the Gracchi brothers from being killed by the senate oligarchy in 133 and 121 BC, so they could help the poor.

I want to feel history.

I want to cross the Rubicon with Julius Caesar, and then scream with him, "*Et tu Brute?*—And you Brutus?" when he was stabbed to death in treachery in 44 BC.

I want to cry with the Romans who stood near his funeral pyre until the flames went out after midnight, and then went home with tears in their eyes, and his ashes as a sacred memento of their dear leader. I want to keep his ashes in my urn.

I want to hear the fourteen Philippics of Cicero against Mark Antony.

I want to feel history.

I want to hold the head of Cicero and read the timidity in his eyes after he was beheaded by the soldiers of Mark Antony while fleeing Rome.

I want to watch Octavian and Agrippa defeat Mark Antony at the battle of Actium in 31 BC. I want to ask Mark Antony why he fled after Cleopatra rather than fighting like a Roman. I want to see the defeated faces of lovers in a suicidal abandon.

I want to feel history.

I want to learn statecraft from Augustus and smell the dirt around his house on Palatine Hill, where he walked before dying in AD 14. I want to enjoy the chariot races in the Circus Maximus looking down from his palace.

I want to feel history.

I want to laugh at the absurdity of Caligula naming his horse a senator. I want to stutter with Claudius, and then play the fiddle with Nero, while Rome was burning.

I want to feel history.

I want to inaugurate the Colosseum with Titus in AD 80, and then feel the pain of a dying gladiator through the whites of his eyes.

I want to feel history.

I want to enjoy the good life under the five philosopher kings from Nerva to Marcus Aurelius, and build the Pantheon with Hadrian in AD 130. I want to see Rome transition from paganism to Christianity with Constantine the Great.

I want to swim in the Tiber and then bathe in the baths of Caracalla.

I want to weep at the fall of Rome in AD 476 when Augustulus abdicated under the barbarian attack, and then beg Odoacer to leave her alone.

I want to hug her at zenith and kiss her at nadir.

I want to feel history.

Today, when I see the ruins of the Roman Forum from Palatine Hill, I want to imagine her grandeur, when Caesar and Cicero walked there.

I want to feel history.

Exhausted, when I fall asleep at night, *Roma* whispers in my ear, "Let us talk history over a glass of wine. You can ask me anything you want."

Then I ask her the secret of her inner beauty, under the filth of cigarette butts stuck between her cobblestones. She answers that more than physical, her beauty is metaphysical. It is as eternal as the idea of Rome. I would have to know the biography of every cobblestone and brick in Rome to understand the secret of her beauty. And then she disappears in the dark.

I cry out: "How do you expect me to embrace eternity when I am finite in time? Why do you want me to hug infinity when I am finite in space?"

Through the wind, she teases, "Come back and see me at twilight. I will tell you over a glass of wine."

I say yes, for the only way to feel history is through the secret of
her beauty.

So, where night dissipates into dawn,

where daylight scatters into twilight,

where facts melt into fiction,

where history dissolves into legend,

I want to feel history.

CHANGE

The soldiers were called baby killers yesterday.
Today they are called heroes.
The draft dodgers of yesteryear
are the leaders of today.
Those who deferred the draft yesterday
are sending kids of others to the front line today
to fight in a rich man's war.
The anti-war movement
was no more than
an anti-draft movement
that ended when the draft ended.
Those who danced on the enemy tanks
in mocking laughter of treason yesterday
are a distant memory
of the Punic War today.
Sons of ghettos, barrios, reservations, mines
were drafted then.
Today they are volunteers,
as if they have a choice.
Then the draft was military.
Today it is economic.
Cannon fodder was cheap yesterday,
today it costs dearly.

My boy is good.
Take that no-good boy
from the wrong side of town.
Let us find all the poor, the exploited,
the downtrodden, the vulnerable,
the precarious, the disenfranchised,
and employ them gainfully
in the military,
so, they can appreciate
how lucky they are
to live in the home of the brave
and the land of the free.
Those with little stake in freedom
are supposed to defend it with their lives,
while those with a stake
can wave Old Glory in the front yard,
and enjoy barbecue and booze in the back.
Let us kick some butts in the desert
to teach those barbarians a lesson.
It is easier to fight wars now
and cheaper in blood
with the have-nots doing the fighting
and no draft to disturb the haves.
It is easier
to make a hero out of someone else's child
than your own.
Better a live coward in the basement
than a dead hero in the desert.
Let the children of others become heroes.
We will put them on a pedestal
and worship them.

Just throw money at them
and they will come.
The chaos in the desert,
millions of refugees
fleeing the wasteland
tailor-made for a democracy,
to die in a no-man's-land,
all in the name of freedom.
One, two, three, four tours
can make the sane insane,
and the insane suicidal.
Basket cases when they leave,
suicidal when they return.
Broken men with broken lives
lumped together
in a huge pile of indifference.
The plebeian is still doing
the dirty work of the patrician.
So we can all enjoy the fruits
of freedom and democracy
in our comfortable numbness
of a good life.
The bourgeoisie says,
don't talk to us about fairness
when what you really want is a class struggle.
Don't talk about justice and equality
when what you really want is a revolution.
My, how things change
while remaining the same.
How beautiful carpets of euphemism
hide the dirty grit of reality.

How garments of sanctimony
cover the body of mendacity.
How well have we mastered
the art of constant reality
behind the fictional facade of change.
A million dead fingers point at us
from a tomb of collective social guilt
behind a chorus of loud screams
Je vous accuse—I accuse you.

LOVE

Where is that young love
wrapped in your beauty,
insulated from reality,
oblivious to tomorrow,
drowning in a pitcher of beer
lost in a ring of cigarette smoke?
In the comfortable life of a caged bird
with freedom a distant thought
where is that young love?
Before bills, mortgage, insurance stole that love,
before lawn mowed that love,
before snow plowed that love,
before leaves raked that love,
in a fictional ideal of a good life,
where is that young love?
Please help me find that love
lost behind the facade
of material security
hollowed out by
the demands of economic metrics
into an empty shell.
Day in and day out
running around in circles

going nowhere
on a stationary bicycle
to spiral around in the futility
of nothingness.
Before fall turns into winter
and the ice freezes the burial ground
please help me find that love.
Chipped away
bit by bit
piece by piece
inch by inch
minute by minute
unbeknownst to everyone
it dissipated
in keeping up with the Joneses
until nothing remained
but gray hair and a frail body
as a sad reminder of a finite life.
Do you remember
the game of hide and seek
we used to play when young?
You used to hide from me
and I used to hide from you
until we dissolved
into an embrace
of youthful abandon
so, no one could find us.
Please help me find that love
high as the mountain
sublime as the blue sky
that no one can reach.

Carefree, vibrant, blind,
grounded in the bliss of ignorance
for which I could run away from life
and melt into your arms.
Please find me that oasis
deep down
in the desert of reality.
So I can go to sleep
beside you
tired of chasing a mirage
with no worries
and no wake-up call
from the alarm clock of life.

SOLITUDE

Please help me find that solitude
shattered by WTOP[2] radio
news, traffic, and weather
into a million pieces
scattered all over the house.
Even if I can put them together
to make the solitude whole again
I cannot swim fast enough
to catch all the ideas
all the dreams
all the thoughts
that escaped
floating downstream
miles away.
I was in a utopian dream
enjoying a cup of tea
tranquil, peaceful, quiet
until the mundane sound
of the radio
shattered the silence
with a sledgehammer of reality.
Traffic jams, shootings, crimes, violence

2. WTOP news, traffic, and weather is a radio station in Washington, DC.

bloodshed being analyzed
in a psychobabble of why.
Same rituals every time
same questions
same prayers
same candlelight vigils
same tear-jerking
same heartbreak
same flowers
same platitudes
from seasoned politicians,
we will get to the bottom of this.
But then what?
What about the next time?
We will worry about that crisis
when it happens.
Different victims
different culprits
different parents
different spouses
different siblings
different children
all members of one large family
mourning the dead
until we all go numb
to the reality around us
to the society we live in
as if all this is the norm.
If you think things are bad here
try living somewhere else.
I voted with my young feet to come here.

I can no longer vote with my tired, old feet.
So give me back the fictional simplicity of solitude
calming, soothing, peaceful
rather than a bombardment of nightmarish news stories.
Let me enjoy my cup of tea
dipped in solitude
for the rest of my days.
Since I cannot
step into the same river twice
please help me find that peace
shattered by WTOP
news, traffic, and weather.

CUES

Dry after a camping trip
in the rain and a ride in the rapids,
a twitch of the face
a roll of the eyes,
missed cues all along
lost in a cultural translation
sometimes unexpected
in the short ride in a car.
From a stunning beauty with a husky voice
created by God in his spare moments,
to an infatuated naive caged bird.
Wasting time with shining gems
with no interest, except to be polite and funny,
a wrong message to the diamond that meant everything.
Hurting you with the young stupidity
and naivete of an alien caged bird,
I tried your patience
and was hurt when rejected
in a swirl of emotions to tear me apart.
A lack of smile expressing my pain
made things worse in a seeming indifference.
We should not try that kind of a thing, you said
when I asked you out on a date.

I enjoyed playing the music on a jukebox
drowning tears in a pitcher of beer
and a cloud of smoke
as bigotry took over the cage.
In a drunken stupor, I failed to talk
and you walked out in anger and disgust.
The only thing this mule understands is a two-by-four
to teach him a lesson.
When the grass was green
my thoughts were pure.
And when the leaves are falling
I am sorry to hurt your feelings.
As the youth was being wasted on the young,
the shortcomings were all mine,
but they were not on purpose.
I have always wished you well
and I still do
despite the deepest cut
as I chase the mirage to grasp your beauty
in a fictional lament over spilt milk.

FROZEN TUNDRA

Born on April Fool's Day
you had warmth rare in a frozen tundra.
An outgoing smile on a bubbly face
you could easily captivate an alien bird.
And the bird fell for your charm,
your long blond hair, your pretty face.
Catholic to the core, you wanted to be a nun
or have a large family
two extremes with no happy medium.
You came out of the tundra to see the bird in a cage.
There is nothing sacred for you guys
you scolded a friend.
Just eat the spaghetti.
You needed to be needed.
What do you want from me?
You asked after a beer in a bar.
Love I said, to ease the life in a cage.
A metaphysical answer
to a physical question.
You were a creature of the tundra
comfortable in your ways.
No compromise with a city boy
so, you went your way back to the tundra,

and the bird flew when the cage opened.
Radiant at dawn,
I hope you are happy at dusk.
I thank you for your sunny outlook
and the time you spent with me
to cheer me up
in the fictional absurdity of cage life.

DECEIT

I still remember
your incredible beauty
wrapped in blue polka dots floating in a sea of white,
your long dark hair neatly cut
flowing down to your waist
in a silky river.
The residual taste of tea
that you poured in a Chinese restaurant
still lingers in my mouth.
One, two, three, four, five phone calls
never conveyed to you
by a friend close as a sister.
Jealous about a forbidden fruit
she could never have
so why should you?
Wily as a fox
she knew her victims well,
and made her treacherous move.
He never called you, no phone call, no nothing.
You believed her, you trusted her
web of lies in a demonic play.
Paralyzed by shyness
assuming the worst

the foreign bird in a cage could not chirp loud enough.
I like you,
I want to be with you,
I want to know you better.
A hundred eyes staring at me
what is wrong with this jerk?
Criticism, innuendoes, demonization
wrapped in bigotry
by fellow caged birds
with no basis in facts
insults, vilification drenched in beer.
No girl is coming to your party
when it is time to leave the cage.
After three years in a cage
the bird wanted to fly as soon as free
to spread his wings in freedom.
No man can go forward in a crystal ball
nor travel back in time.
What seemed important in the spring
is so irrelevant in the fall.
And what is important in the fall
seemed so irrelevant in the spring.
All I can do in the twilight
with your beauty frozen in my mind
is apologize for not being assertive
and purge my heart of guilt
at a different intersection of space and time
in a fictional articulation of tears.

A BLOODY FRIDAY

I want to wipe tears from the eyes
of the Statue of Liberty.
Then swim across the Atlantic Ocean
to heal the wounds of a beauty
soaked in blood.
Paris, my love
I am sorry I could not be with you
in your darkest hour of need,
when you were being shot
by barbarians
grounded in religious bigotry
biting the hand that feeds.
Smoldering with anger and hatred towards
your carefree, vibrant life.
They wanted to put you in a veil
to subject you to the life
of a desert tribe
and live in the fifteenth century
like the slave of a fanatic
who chops off heads of infidels
that do not agree.
Too cowardly to fight on the battlefield
he brought the battle to you

to kill the innocent
enjoying the carefree Friday evening
and drench you in a pool of blood.
Six separate wounds
one more severe than the other.
Blood was not dry on Charlie Hebdo
when the blood bath came to Bataclan
to the heart of liberty, equality, fraternity
from those bent on destroying them.
A chorus of screams inside
apocalypse wrapped in chaos.
Help us, protect us, rescue us
they are shooting us like birds.
Innocent youth against cold blood
shocking enough to create paralyzing numbness.
Wake up humanity, it is time to fight
the barbarity of jihadi terrorism.
We will not let you destroy
the carefree, vibrant beauty of Paris.
We will not let you defeat
the soul of civilization.
We will not let you drag
liberty, equality, fraternity
into the mud and blood of your savage creation.
We will not give up.
We will not give in.
We will not succumb.
And when we win
the entire humanity will climb
the Arc de Triomphe
in red, white, and blue

singing La Marseillaise
to shout at the top of her lungs
for every barbarian to hear it
loud and clear.
Vive la liberté!
Vive la fraternité!
Vive l'égalité!
Vive la France!
Vive Paris!
And then go to bed tired
in a slumber of peaceful abandon.
Rest assured
we will prevail, my love.

FRENCH

Like a beautiful woman
you elude me.
The moment I think I caught you
you escape from my fingers with a boisterous laugh.
With half of you silent
unlike Spanish and German
you are invisible to an untrained ear
and difficult to fathom.
Your complex grammar
full of rules boggles my mind.
Why can't you be simple like English
with fewer rules and fewer conjugations
with no *le,* and no *la*
with no *accent aigu, grave* or *circonflex*?
Why do your beauty and richness
come with such a heavy price
to discourage the fainthearted
and fool the brave?
Despite your thorny grammar
that comes with the beautiful rose
I love you my dear princess
for your stunning beauty of *liaisons* and *élisions*
that flow like a smooth river with deep undercurrents

and for your rich versatility.
I want to spend more time with you
to know you better
and to get close to you
over a bottle of wine.
For French, you are the love of my life.

PARIS

(A love poem)
Like a fictional outpost of history
in spirit, if not in the flesh
I am always with you.
I was here in 250 BC
when the hardy Celtic people settled on the Seine.
You were marshy then,
so, they named you Leukteih.
I was here in 52 BC
when Julius Caesar came to town
and Romans Latinized you to Lutetia.
They called the Gallic tribe Parisii.
I was here in the third century,
when you were renamed *Civitas Parisiorum*—City of Parisii.
I rejoiced in AD 360
when you finally became Paris.
I carried the red flag of the revolution in 1789,
and witnessed the guillotine drop on Marie Antoinette in 1793.
Then the revolution devoured 1200 souls
including her sons
Robespierre and Danton in 1794.
I laughed off the self-coronation of Napoleon
to the dismay of the Pope in 1804,

and cried at Waterloo in 1815
when fortune turned on him.
I was sad for you in 1871
when the Paris Commune was suppressed,
and 20,000 brave souls perished.
I was proud of you in 1889
when 2 million people came to see
your tower of steel built by Gustav Eiffel.
I breathed a sigh of relief when the war to end all wars ended,
and the Treaty of Versailles was signed
in the Hall of Mirrors in 1919.
I spread roses on the tomb at Arc de Triomphe
when the Unknown Soldier was buried in 1920.
I shouted *Vive la France!*
when de Gaulle entered Paris in 1944
to mark the end of another bloody war.
Today, I would love to live with you in the flesh
if I were rich.
But I am not,
so, I can only see you from time to time.
Before twilight dissolves into the abyss of darkness
I want to be with you.
In the stillness of the night
when the street noise does not hammer my thoughts,
and the cobwebs do not clutter my mind,
I want to listen to your heartbeat through the cobblestones.
I hugged you in Latin in the Latin Quarter.
Now I want to kiss you in French on the Left Bank.
I want to drink your beauty with my eyes
until it becomes part of me,
and stays with me forever.

I want to synchronize with your rhythm
until the resonance breaks me down.
Now that I am home
I miss your pulse.
I miss walking along the Champs-Élysée,
and climbing the Eiffel Tower.
I miss the majesty of Arc de Triomphe,
and listening to mass at Notre-Dame
that sounds beautiful in French.
I miss the modern art trapped in the steel web of the Pompidou
Center,
and spending endless hours under the pyramid of the Louvre
to be with Mona Lisa and Venus de Milo.
I miss the *Bateaux Mouches*[3] on the Seine.
I think of you in solitude,
and long for you.
For Paris
I love you.

3. *Bateaux Mouches* are open excursion boats on the river Seine in Paris.

GOD

You can keep your morose god
who never laughed in his life
and died for your sins
so, you can live an eternal life
in a fictional heaven
that no one has ever seen.
You can keep your desert god
destroying apostates
who enslaves your mother, sister, daughter, wife
in a labyrinth of harems wrapped in a veil
with a name without a face
reducing half of humanity
to a subhuman level.
You can keep your mountain god
who gave ten commandments
to his prophet
that are impossible to follow
by any human being
dead or alive.
I have no use for a god
whose praying disciples
with a divine calling of celibacy
prey on poor, innocent children

in a silent conspiracy
of a religious hierarchy
under a vow of poverty,
or a god whose children
are born unequal
in an inhuman construct
of a rigid caste system
sanctioned by a divine apartheid
that good deeds may never transcend
in countless reincarnations.
Give me instead a god I can relate to
a happy god who can make me happy
a dancing god who can make me dance
a singing god who can make me sing
a drinking god who can make me drink.
Give me a god of reason and knowledge
I can understand and debate
not a god of faith or obedience
that must be believed or obeyed
without question
in mindless conformity.
Give me a god
who can create a heaven on earth
we can all enjoy, while still alive
not a god who keeps us miserable here
with a false promise of a happy hereafter.
Give me a finite god I can see
not an infinite god I cannot,
a god who can answer my questions
not a god I can never talk to
over a glass of beer.

Give me a god whose potent opiate
drowns the agony of life
in a sea of ecstasy,
a god who can love humanity
in an embrace of eternal bliss.
Since I cannot find a religion
that does not kill in the name of god
find me a god
who does not kill in the name of religion.

IF ONLY FOR ONE DAY

If only for one day
I want to live without you
to feel solitude without loneliness
idleness without laziness
to experience again
a slice of that single life
long forgotten
long forsaken
extricated from the mothballs of the past.
I want to live that life again
with careless abandon
if only for one day.
I want to browse books
in a book store, in a library.
I want to read
insulated from the clutter of noise,
to think
isolated from the demands of an agenda,
to write
about the fictitious footprints we may leave behind
on the pragmatic sands of nonfiction
if only for one day.
I want to kiss you

with no chains of commitment,
hug you
with no reins of responsibility.
I want to breathe freedom
on the margins of our marriage
if only for one day.
Tomorrow, I promise
I will return to the fold
with all the commitments,
all the responsibilities,
all the quid pro quo,
all the agendas intact,
without missing a beat,
as if today never happened.
But today,
I want to chase the mirage of love
with no strings attached,
in the soulless desert of life
without you
if only for one day.

SOMEDAY

Someday . . .
You, my friend, and I
with Sartre and Camus in Les Deux Magots[4]
will discuss absurdity, nothingness, and the nausea of human existence
over a cigar, a bottle of wine, a *croque monsieur*, and a *croque madame*,
in the charming quarter of Saint-Germain-des-Prés.
Comfortably numb
we will romanticize poverty
and shed a few crocodile tears
for hunger and destitution in the third world,
with imported sentiments and borrowed emotions
we will pontificate in poems,
divorced from the subjective feel for reality.
We will philosophize in plays
to rationalize their misery
and intellectualize ours.
But today . . .
bitten by the constant buzz of mosquitoes
swatting the flies with *No Exit*[5] excreting on the food
suffocated by clouds of cigarette smoke

4. Les Deux Magots is a famous café in Paris.
5. *The Flies* and *No Exit* are plays by Jean-Paul Sartre.

47

we live in the darkness of the third world
watching ladies of the night flaunting their wares
in the broad daylight
smoking, drinking, cursing their fate
under the scorching sun.
Beyond the wasteland of nothingness,
where hope is a cruel joke,
and individual screams dissolve into a collective yawn,
to attract the customers urinating nearby,
a few rupees of fun for a death in a leaky hut.
In a fast-moving crowded train
suffocating with the human exhaust and condensate
of oppressive heat,
insulated from their reality
of a slaughterhouse,
lives too old, too broken, too exhausted
to push the rock of Sisyphus[6]
over the mount of absurdity.
Too young to be fired, too poor to quit,
too wretched to die with dignity.
We hear their outcry
without listening to their tears
begging for freedom from the nausea of existence.
Embracing fatalistic inaction
we pontificate,
we philosophize,
with Sartre and Camus,
with imported philosophy and borrowed ideas,
fitting a square peg of poverty in a round hole of affluence
in the futility of geometric fiction.

6. "The Myth of Sisyphus" is a philosophical essay by Albert Camus.

With no subjective feel for reality
we discuss a solution
without defining the problem.
Humans dropping like flies
we pull their dead bodies out of rivers
to cremate them like dogs
among melting pipes of a crematorium
under the heat overload
in an indifferent jungle flooded with tears of weeping willows
singing the religious chant in a monotone.
But someday
I promise you
my dear friend
we will vote with our feet
and go to Les Deux Magots
to join Sartre and Camus
to romanticize poverty
over a cigar, a bottle of wine
a *croque monsieur* and a *croque madame*
with imported sentiments and borrowed emotions
we will suffocate in the web of affluence
comfortably numb
and divorced from hunger
shed a few crocodile tears
waiting for Godot[7] to create a utopia
Someday . . .

7. *Waiting for Godot* is a play by Samuel Beckett.

PONDICHERRY

My darling
lives in Pondicherry.
I'm home alone
in the coronavirus prison
but she is far from here.
She can't be here
and I can't be there.
I miss her a lot
because I love my darling.
That is the tragedy of Pondicherry.
When it snows here
and it is cold,
I am skiing.
She swims in the Indian Ocean
where the weather is nice.
I've never been there
and I will never go there
although
great is
the temptation of Pondicherry.
I can practice my French
with her
and she can practice her English

with me
because we speak both in Pondicherry.
Fictitious love of real people
is a sandcastle
built on the mirage.
So, I suffer in America
and kiss the air
while my dear, of course
has fun in Pondicherry.

TO POSTERITY

If and when you judge me
which I am sure you will
please judge my words in my language
lest they should lose context in yours.
Please judge me in my *zeitgeist*[8]
not in yours.
Please judge me in my space and time
not in yours.
Please judge me in my framework
not in yours.
Please judge me in my technology
not in yours.
For I will appear backward in your technology
just as my ancestors looked in mine,
and as you will seem to your posterity.
And before you get smug in your moral superiority,
and confound your woke political correctness with morality
superseding reality,
face me with your intellectual castle controlling your emotions
rather than confront me with your emotional redoubt in control
of your reason.
Listen to my logic

8. *Zeitgeist* is the spirit of the age.

before you drown me out in your emotional diatribe.
Put my assets and liabilities on the balance
along with my gains and losses
before throwing the baby out with the bathwater.
Appreciate my virtue as much as you condemn my vice
and before you cancel me out from your collective memory
be humble enough to realize
that your posterity may cancel you out
with no less ferocity
and no more fairness.

LIFE

Jesus Christ
a crucifix
a crown of thorns
was that life?

LIBERTY

Children killing children
fourteen, fifteen, sixteen
with assault rifles
that belong in a combat zone
blood splattered in classrooms, hallways
dead bodies everywhere.
Screams of help us
someone is shooting,
kids are dying,
chaos, confusion, running,
someone call 911.
Liberty to maintain self-defense
under an irrational anachronism
degenerates into frequent mass shootings,
spilling the blood of young and old, men and women.
A bullet does not discriminate.
It does the job
of bleeding you to death.
Go to school happy
and come back in a body bag.
Tears of parents' dissolve
into the blood of their children.
Where are our children?

Are they safe?
We do not know yet.
Once police secure the building
we will look for the victims.
Institutions of learning
turning into armed camps
and killing fields.
Children dying before their first kiss,
their first hug, their first love,
too young to lose innocence,
all under the pretext of liberty.
Cruel *schadenfreude*[9] with a laughing emoji[10]
boisterous laughter in a pool of blood
of classmates, we played with yesterday.
We do not care about your right to life, liberty, and the pursuit of happiness
as long as we keep our right to bear arms.
Freedom without discipline,
rights without responsibility,
law without order or justice,
resulting in anarchy.
No place is safe today
from gun violence.
Reason overpowered by madness, greed, and ambition,
citizens are helpless.
Cries fall on deaf ears.
Sighs dissipate into numbness.
Tears condense into indifference.
Another prayer, another candlelight vigil,

9. *Schadenfreude* is malicious gloating.
10. An icon used in electronic communication to add subtle emotional emphasis to a sentence in text.

more flowers, more tears, more platitudes,
words devoid of action
with no results,
then back to the status quo
before another shooting on the evening news
ABC, CBS, NBC, CNN.
So, what else is new today
in the home of the brave
and the land of the free?

AN UNFINISHED POEM

This is an unfinished poem
like our love and our lives,
like an incomplete statue emerging from the amorphous marble,
buried under material wants
disguised as emotional needs,
insignificant many
overwhelming the significant few
confusing goals with activities.
In a finite life
before time runs out
and we say goodbye
to the world we live in
I would like to finish this poem
with a simple life
focused on needs
rather than wants
on happiness
rather than commodities
on a significant few rather than insignificant many.
Like the birth pangs of a finished statue
born from the amorphous marble of love
before passing into oblivion.
I will leave behind a beautiful poem
for posterity.

9/11

Wife in New York City for work
Daughter in first grade at school
Is mommy dead? she asked.
No honey, I said, she is alive.

THE LOST POEM

"Ma petite rose"
the poem I wrote for you
in my French class
"My little rose"
was lost in a pile of papers
perhaps shredded to death in a paper shredder
or dissolved into the solvent of recyclables
by mistake.
No matter how hard I try,
I cannot find the lost poem
any more than I can find the lost love
that was an illusion at dawn
and is a mirage at dusk
drowned by the turbulence of life
in the river of time
that I can fathom no more.
The poem that made me laugh
when you laughed
and cry when you cried.
The poem that made me happy
when you were happy
and sad when you were sad.
The poem that wiped your tears

with hugs and kisses.
The poem to penetrate your heart
and reach the core of your love
is unfortunately no more.
I am sorry my little rose
but it is lost forever
in an abyss of time.

A MONUMENT TO LOVE

No one will build
a beautiful symmetrical monument dedicated
to our love,
as Shahjahan, the Mughal emperor built
for his favorite queen Mumtaz Mahal,
the crown of the palace.
No one will call our monument
a tear-drop on the cheek of time,
as Tagore called the Taj Mahal
to write a poem exalting the love of the rich and the powerful.
For our eternal monument
instead of white marble and red sandstone
will be built with tears and laughter,
hugs and kisses of commoners
that exalts all love
without disparaging any.
That dissects the human heart to find love
rather than wealth and power,
that wipes tears on the cheeks of real humans
rather than on the cheek of time.
It will be an asymmetrical monument
devoid of beautiful symmetry
to celebrate the imperfect love

of imperfect people
at different frequencies
trying to synchronize the asynchronous.
Our monument, being metaphysical
unlike the Taj
will not be ephemeral,
for it can never be destroyed.
It will be our gift to posterity
from here to eternity.
My dear, I promise you
it will last forever
to embrace infinity.

THE RAPE[11]

When the big boy raped the little girl,
we gave her food, shelter, clothing, medicine, weapons.
We discussed, debated, pontificated.
We pleaded, negotiated with the rapist
not to rape the little girl.
We condemned, sanctioned, passed resolutions
to punish the rapist.
We even told him what we will and will not do
to save the little girl.
Failing to dissuade the perpetrator, however,
we hid behind the collective cowardice of technicalities
to let the cooler heads prevail,
and did little to stop the rapist.
The girl, naked, soaked in blood, cried out,
help me, help me, stop the rape.
But insulated from her reality,
we witnessed it in gut-wrenching detail,
and hesitated in a dither,
so, he could rape more.
It is one thing to rape an unallied girl,
but if you dare touch an allied one,
we will fight you with everything we have.

11. Russian attack on Ukraine on February 24, 2022.

The reckless mediocrity laughed,
wrapping mendacity in subterfuge
blamed the girl
and continued raping,
calling it consensual
in an Orwellian doublespeak.

FOURTH OF JULY

On Independence Day
we listened to the national anthem,
watched the parades with patriotic pride and joy,
enjoyed the rock concert,
feasted before the fireworks,
watched another mass shooting on television,
and then waved American flags,
made in communist China.

1/6

The attack on the US Capitol
by an angry, unruly mob
in a violent insurrection in a democracy
they did not create,
to overturn an election
decided by a majority,
fair and square
that did not please the minority.
Throw out the rule of law,
we are the law.
If we do not like the result
we will change it with violence.
We will replace the ballot with bullets
to get what we want.
Hang the VP, kill the Speaker,
get rid of all the enemies
and obstacles that interfere.
We want to replace an experiment in democracy
with an autocracy of our design.
We want to destroy the Republic to save America
and destroy the democracy to save the constitution
like a war to end all wars.
The hell with decency, fairness, and due process,

for we are the patriots.
We decide what is right and what is wrong,
what is good and what is bad.
Inspired by our leader,
we will smash your heads
with our flag poles
if you try to stop us.
Life, liberty, and the pursuit of happiness
hanging by a noose wrapped in bigotry
of a personality cult,
in the home of the brave and the land of the free.
It can never happen here, we said,
but it is happening here
in front of our eyes
for the entire world to see
in dismay and disbelief.
Founding Fathers are turning in their graves with fear
at the anarchy, the chaos, and the rule of the king mob.
After more than two hundred years of democracy
are we ready to govern ourselves
in a government by the consent of the governed?
"What have we got, doctor,"
someone asked outside Independence Hall,
"a republic or a monarchy?"[12]
"A republic it is,"
said the Founding Father
with an ominous smile,
"if you can keep it."

12. Benjamin Franklin was called "doctor" due to his distinguished accomplishments in many areas.

A PARENTHESIS

Please do not ignore
a word in a parenthesis
if it is less relevant than the one outside.
Please do not underestimate a life in a parenthesis
if it is less glamorous than the one outside.
In a paradox of a parenthesis
in and out may trade places anytime.
What is glamorous today
may lose its glamour tomorrow,
and what is relevant today
may become irrelevant tomorrow.
What is outside the parenthesis
maybe more ephemeral
than what is inside.
So, in respect of a parenthesis
value what outlives
the transitory life
of wealth, power, and glory.
Add value to the world you live in
to enrich posterity
in the metaphysical space
if not in the physical one.
And it will thank you
for a life well lived in a parenthesis.

SEMPRE IMPARO

At the age of eighty-seven
Michelangelo said in humility
Ancora imparo—I am still learning.
Excuse me, sir, I said
I admire your passionate curiosity
but did you mean to say *sempre imparo*—I am always learning?

A GHAZAL[13]

(A mirage in search of an oasis)
Since you wanted me to write you a graceful ghazal
I finally wrote for you this thoughtful ghazal.
When the prosaic desert of life reached the poetic oasis of love
the desert rose promised bliss if I wrote her a beautiful ghazal.
Then I gave her five couplets of my wonderful ghazal
and she complained, this is only half, where is the full ghazal?
Urdu being so romantic and English being so pragmatic
how do I translate Urdu ambiance into a meaningful ghazal?
To regret the love lost is crying over spilt milk
all I can do today is write you a hopeful ghazal.
As our love dissolved in a glass of wine and a pitcher of beer
the cleric called our intoxication a sinful ghazal.
When God banished Adam and Eve from the garden of Eden
he abandoned humanity in a vengeful ghazal.
As she saw the priest drinking in the house of wine
the barmaid felt sorry and prayed in a merciful ghazal.
Do not be so serious and drink some wine, said the barmaid
on a deathbed, a life is no more than a wasteful ghazal.
When you are happy, cheerful, and laughing
I dissolve your laughter into mine in a joyful ghazal.
And when you are sad, morose, and crying

13. A *ghazal* is a love poem bound by refrain and rhyme.

I wipe your tears with mine in a tearful ghazal.
Thanks for leaving your footprints on my life, Ma
I follow them everywhere in a wistful ghazal.
The pain of your deep cut is still fresh in my heart
now I chase the mirage of love in a wishful ghazal.
Many have rejected me before and after you
what hurts more is you cut me with a woeful ghazal.
As the rings of smoke dissipated our love in prejudice
I looked for the villain who wrote that artful ghazal.
Bigotry has no room for intelligence, talent, or ability
it destroys all merit outside the box in a spiteful ghazal.
Since the news shattered my solitude into a million pieces
I am trying to put them together in a peaceful ghazal.
Life is too short for gloom and doom, my friend
Just take it easy, and write me a cheerful ghazal.
As the river of ghazal kept overflowing and knew no bounds
I swam in the deep emotional currents of a bountiful ghazal.
Do not let it go to your head Rohit, this awful ghazal
read Mir and Ghalib[14] to see life as a painful ghazal.

14. Mir and Ghalib were great Urdu poets.

A MIRAGE AND AN OASIS

(A tribute to a fellow traveler)
On a starry night
you my friend and I
two gypsies
in the destitute darkness
dreamt of reaching the full moon
ten thousand miles away
like a fictional outpost of reality
to escape the emotional oasis
in a material desert beyond the superfluous wasteland
wrapped in a mirage of hope.
Mistaking an oasis for a mirage
and a mirage for an oasis
we marched on in a desert full of camels
and climbed mountains full of goats
trying to reach the peak
with our fellow travelers
against the headwinds of overwhelming odds
calibrating the compass when we fell down
lest we should lose the way.
Our paths diverged
into worlds of different currencies
losing the physical touch

but not the metaphysical link.
The river of time kept flowing before our eyes
unbeknownst to us in an absent-minded daze
while idle thoughts filled the empty hours.
In the fog of twilight
when we reached the material oasis
it was wrapped in an emotional mirage
of a cynical desert beyond the superficial wasteland.
What made the journey worthwhile
my friend
was the mirage
that propelled us forward to the oasis
with the constant force of a tailwind.

MEMENTO MORI

Before I bask in the glory
of a victorious Roman general
marching through the streets of Rome
towards the Temple of Jupiter on the Capitoline Hill
to thank him for the victory
and to sacrifice the vanquished
on a crucifix,
please whisper in my ear
memento mori—remember death.
Before I forget that I have only one life
and squander my time on insignificant many
rather than on a significant few
please whisper in my ear
memento mori—remember death.
Before I melt in your arms
and dissolve into the darkness of a starry night
to watch the life passing by in the sky
with an absent-minded incredulity,
please whisper in my ear
memento mori—remember death.
In the twilight of my life,
if I am too angry to love you
and to wipe your tears when you hurt,

please whisper in my ear
memento mori—remember death.
If I ever feel arrogant and indispensable
before you bury me in a graveyard
of indispensables,
please whisper in my ear
memento mori—remember death.
In the indestructible moments of my zenith
if I forget the inevitable,
please remind me of the finitude
of our lives together
and the fragility of our love,
then please whisper in my ear
memento mori—remember death.

CARPE DIEM!

Age compels us to appreciate
the shortness of our lives,
that youth was indestructible
but that age is fragile.
It seems like we just met yesterday,
married yesterday,
had our child yesterday,
loved yesterday,
laughed and cried yesterday.
The dawn was only yesterday
but today is already dusk.
The entire day passed us by in a dream,
like life condensed in a wink.
What remains is even less.
The twilight will soon dissipate into darkness
as we dissolve into an abyss.
Given only one life
to live, to love, to laugh, to cry,
to add value to the world we live in
for the posterity to inherit,
to make a difference
in an indifferent universe
with time getting more precious every day

that we can ill afford to waste
on a diffused focus.
Every idle moment
every lazy instinct
steals from what is left
as Horace reminds us
with a whisper in our ears
Carpe diem!
Seize the day!

AMOR FATI

In the battle of fate and destiny
of free will and determinism
the stoic tells me to love my fate—*amor fati*.
Do not regret the past,
accept the present as it is,
whatever happens, is for the best.
Do not fight what is beyond your control
Premeditatio mallorum—premeditate the evils,
prepare for the worst, but hope for the best,
play the best game you can with the cards you are dealt.
Beyond that just love your fate.
But how does one separate fate from destiny?
How does one know what is subject to free will
and what is predetermined?
What is within our control
and what is not?
How does one learn from the past
never to repeat the mistakes
if one embraces the fatalism
of loving fate?
As only action can change reality,
how does one change the inaction of fate
into the action of destiny?

As acceptance of fate is reactive
while the choice of destiny is proactive,
how can one resign to fate
and yet add value
to the world, one lives in?
How can one make a difference
in the indifference of the universe?
How can one answer Nietzsche[15]
when he asks, who wants to be my fate?
Sorry sir, I am too busy with destiny
to worry about fate.

15. Friedrich Nietzsche (1844–1900) was a German philosopher.

NON OMNIS MORIAR

(A poem wrapped in a testament)
My dear wife and daughter
I will pass into oblivion
as everyone must,
since no one lasts forever.
I will go from ashes to ashes, from dust to dust
and metamorphose into the inanimate.
To continue living thereafter
the concrete must dissolve into the abstract
in spaces that belong to the living.
Through my prose and poems
I will live
to add value to posterity
spending my remaining days
in pursuit of ideas.
Transcending space and time,
thoughts will be my monument to posterity,
as a reminder that I was here.
Rest assured my dears
I will not totally perish.
A part of me will always remain
through the currency of ideas.
As a finite residue of an infinite wish,
not all of me will die—*non omnis moriar.*

THE LAST POEM

Before the emotional lava hardens on the asphalt of reason
I want to write this last poem to you
my dear.
Before the plaque settles in my brain
to destroy my memory,
so, I forget what you look like,
and cannot recognize your beauty anymore.
Before your hugs and kisses
become a foreign gesture,
and your love a borrowed sentiment.
Before I bury the distorted dreams
and broken lives
in a pile of rubble.
Before I wipe your tears,
and erase your sighs.
Before I laugh when you laugh,
and cry when you cry.
Before I forget
the meaning of hugs and kisses.
Before I collapse at the horizon
chasing the mirage of love.
Before I cannot write from

the emotional underground anymore.
I want to hug and kiss you in this last poem of mine
dedicated to you.

ACKNOWLEDGEMENTS

My dear wife Beverly
and my dear daughter Nina
I thank you
for editing my poems with diligence
dotting every i and crossing every t,
connecting the missing dots
and adding rhythm and resonance.
I thank you
for being a poetic oasis
in the prosaic desert of my life,
for navigating the nuances of software
in uploading my book to the internet,
for taking care of the insignificant many
so, I could focus on a significant few.
And before I pass from the scene,
I thank you
for all the hugs and kisses,
for all the tears and laughter, we shared
without which
life would be reduced to mere existence.
And last but not least
I thank you
for being an indispensable part of my life,

for your love and your beauty.
My dear wife and my dear daughter,
I cannot see life without you,
you are my *raisons d'être*.

www.ingramcontent.com/pod-product-compliance
Lightning Source LLC
Chambersburg PA
CBHW062018040426
42447CB00010B/2042